MW00777368

THE HEART AND SOUL OF BLACK WOMEN

Poems of Love, Struggle and Resilience

To: Arlan
Thank you for you
authenticy & vulnerability!
Janet

Janet Autherine

THE HEART AND SOUL OF BLACK WOMEN: POEMS OF LOVE, STRUGGLE AND RESILIENCE

Copyright @2020 by Autherine Publishing
Visit us on the Web at www.JanetAutherine.com
ISBN: 978-0-9912000-6-1

Library of Congress Control Number: 2020915995

All rights reserved. No part of this publication may be reproduced, stored in a retrieval system or transmitted in any form or by an means, electronic, mechanical, photocopying, recording, or otherwise (for commercial purposes), except for brief quotations in printed reviews, without written consent of the publisher. To obtain permission, contact us at JanetAutherine@gmail.com. Copyright @JanetAutherine. Printed in the United States of America (Orlando, FL). September 5, 2020. First edition

THE HEART AND SOUL OF BLACK WOMEN

TO MY SISTERS

My sisters, we are strong and vulnerable and resilient and powerful and full of humanity. We are the dream of our ancestors. We deserve to hold our heads high, showing all sides of our humanity. Our hearts break and mend and break and mend and heal. We don't always bounce back for adversity as fast as we are expected to; we sometimes need therapy and an extra dose of love. As a matter of fact, we need deep and abiding love. We need love without having to struggle, without having to prove ourselves worthy, without having to be the "ride or die" girl. Love, loyalty and respect just because we have a beautiful soul. We are not sacrificial lambs; we need to take care of ourselves so that we can be whole, so that we can be our best selves for our families, show up confidently and take up space in this world. When you look in the mirror, see your majesty, see all the beauty that is inside of you. The world may not alway see us so allow the light of self-love to shine brightly.

These Poems are a mirror to our hearts - love, struggle, strength, vulnerability and resilience.

Roar to your own beat!
Janet

Also by Janet Autherine

Wild Heart, Peaceful Soul: Poems and
Inspiration to Live and Love Harmoniously

Island Mindfulness: How to Use the Transformational
Power of Mindfulness to Create an Abundant Life.

THE HEART AND SOUL OF BLACK WOMEN

Poems of Love, Struggle & Resilience

Mothers of Black Boys Don't Exhale

Mothers of black boys survive by
pushing fear down so it doesn't
overflow, overwhelm our senses
paralyze us and derail our ability
to love, nurture and protect our
black boys

We cling. One hand on the bible
and another holding on to our sons
They say that we love boys and raise girls
Forgive us; we have been anxious since
their birth; we haven't exhaled
because we remember Emmitt Till and
we are in the same prayer circle as the
mothers of Tamir, Elijah, and Trayvon

We embrace the legend of the strong black
woman during the day but cry silent tears at night
As we push down, there is an uprising of fibroids,
anxiety, depression, high blood
pressure, yet we carry on
We organize and fight and vote
and hold our boys close
We fight for our sons because we
need the world to heal
so that every mother of black
boys can finally exhale

A Vulnerable Start to Life

The journey in the womb
is not the same for everyone
Some desperately wanted
to escape the pollution,
the anxiety,
the helplessness
The cutting of the cord
was a gift,
a glimmer of hope
Born vulnerable
Born fighting
Still vulnerable
Still fighting

The Soul of a Black Woman

I am a black woman
Don't look beyond me
Don't see through me
Look me in the eye
Hold my gaze
Listen to my heart
See my soul
See me for who I am, not
what you would like me to be
Accept or reject but don't hide
from my truth

Brown Girl Joy

Brown girl joy is feeling the spirit of
my ancestors rising up in me
It is living in gratitude for the hedge of
protection that they have placed around me
Jamaica, Ghana, Nigeria, Cameroon,
Congo, Mali, Benin & Togo,
Liberia, Sierra Leone…
I recognize your footprints and
proudly walk in them
Our history will never be erased;
your spirit lives on

Black Love

My brother, come as perfectly imperfect as you are
Let us lay a foundation together
Bring working hands and integrity
I will bring loyalty and support
Together, we will gather the materials,
get our hands dirty and build a life together,
brick by brick

Hell No

She looked in the mirror
and realized that she was seeing herself
through someone else's eyes
Will he like my hair, my nose, my attitude
Is my smile perfect enough? Is my joy too bold?
If my love for him overflows and escapes
my lips, will he run from all that I am?
She stripped naked, shaved her head
and dared the world to ask her why

You are Worthy

My sisters, speak your truth
Embrace and love your whole being
Fiercely guard your heart
Be weary of anyone controlling
your life in the name
of God, the devil and everything in between

Clothe yourself in optimism
Banish all forms of negative energy
Take time for mental and physical healthcare
Self-care is Life-care
Proudly recognize that you are the President,
CEO and Keynote Speaker of your life
Nothing important to you works
without a healthy you
You are worthy of love, worthy of abundance and
worthy of a healthy life
Always

The Black Woman's Burden

You don't see the weight on her shoulders but I do
She is silently suffering through years of
verbal abuse,
sexual abuse,
abandonment,
stolen self-esteem,
hidden depression,
suppressed anxiety,
labeled - gold digger, angry, aggressive,
forced to grow up too quickly
All universal issues if she was
valued as a human being
that needs love and protection and kindness and
patience, and room to be sad, happy, angry, joyful
but like her mother, grandmother
and generations of women
before her, she is labeled only as
the strong black woman
So she is having a breakdown all by herself

Some call it the black woman's burden because
she learned early how to silently
cry, scream, breathe with heaving chest,
fall to her knees,
splash water on her face with shaking hands,
absorb the pain,
hit the wall without it making a sound,
then pull in her stomach,
arch her back and stand tall
Face the world with a smile
Hey girl, it's all good
Back to being the life of the office,
lover of broken men,
fixer to all mankind,
lest they add another label — angry black woman

But know that if the pain lives inside,
it becomes a cancer to its host
and travels to the next generation
of strong black women
So fight for yourself
Speak your truth
Let the sound of your voice echo in their ears
You are long overdue for a "meltdown"
Your meltdown is your uprising

Raise Hell

Someone doesn't have to die
for there to be a burial
We bury hopes
We bury dreams
We bury our pain
Try not to take up too much space
Be too joyful
Dream too big
The real burial will come
Your window is now
To rise
Live out loud
Love madly
Claim your space
Raise hell while still alive
Add meaning to your name

Girls Learn Early to Be Resilient

You own the house in which
her heart fearfully resides
Her heart wraps itself around
you in search of safety but
knows that loving you is like
a foster child who never feels
comfortable unpacking her bags
When she feels the rug
being pulled out from under her
heart, she doesn't panic
She has become resilient
She knows how to bounce
back from abandonment
She knows that her heart always
has to be prepared to find a new home

Clothed in Love

I sew a garment with love
It keeps me warm
It reminds me that I matter
It reminds me of my best day
It fits me regardless of my size
It can cover me from head to toe with peace

The hood goes up to drown out negativity,
hide from a bad hair day,
find peace when the mind is overwhelmed,
and to bask in the feel and sound of silence

It is stitched with threads of hope
It covers a broken heart, abuse, disappointments
It provides comfort when I am feeling "less than"
It keeps me warm when the world gets cold

The garment of love knows what my heart needs
It is stitched with the fabric of my life
and it makes me feel as whole as
the day before I was born —
the day before I faced the world
and first cried out in pain

Breaking News! I am Above it All

Today, I forgot to breathe.
The air was suspended between
my throat and nose
Frozen in anticipation of...
war and death,
famine and starvation,
rape and murder,
pride and pain,
fear and gridlock,
spam and debt,
depression and loneliness,
sadness and tears

Tomorrow, I will turn off
the radio,
the television,
the internet,
negative people

Instead, I will take flight
above the clouds
where the air is thin
and I don't have to remind myself to breathe.
I will just look out the window
of life as it crashes by,
descending only when I am in control
of each breath, each heartbeat, each emotion—
Everything that has meaning

Pour Love into the Offering Plate

She will walk into welcoming arms
or be content to sit in solitude
Her hands are weathered from a lifetime of service
Always extended to hug, care for,
toil, fix every broken spirit
For now, they will rest by her side
sometimes hanging freely,
sometimes fist clenched,
sometimes resting protectively on her heart,
sometimes joined together in prayer
Ready to serve again for the warm
embrace of appreciation

A Mother's Prayer for her Gifted Sons

For boys on the autism spectrum
For boys with unique gifts from the universe
I fall to my knees in fervent prayer to the
God of Moses and David and our ancestors
A prayer to heal the hearts and open the minds
of those in the world who are
not conscious enough
to recognize the beauty that is within you
I pray that our entire community
will know the truth
that your difference is not a deficiency
I pray because your light of
greatness remains unseen,
so I must pour wisdom into you and
anoint you with knowledge

I must ask the ancestors for
extra protection for you
and hope that my works and
my prayers are enough
to stop the bullying, for your
contributions to never be
underestimated by teachers and administrators,
for your talents to be recognized by employers,
for law enforcement and those
who hold positions of
power to always see your humanity
and treat you with kindness
I fall on my knees in fervent
prayers to protect you from
a world that pretends to celebrate
uniqueness but won't always
see how grand you are.

Selling Love in the Craft Market

Blanket spread beautifully on the ground
Precious treasures, meticulously handcrafted
and offered with a smile
Touched, admired, test driven but no takers
Price decreased as the hours increased

Treasures to her, trinkets to others
Offered at a premium, not worth it
Offered at a discount, worth questioned
Offered for free, nothing needed
Negotiations failed

The sister in the craft market packed up her wares,
placed the basket on her head and walked away
Another ship arrives tomorrow
Another chance for someone to see
the value in her treasures
Her treasures are precious even
if she is the only one
who values them
Hope restored

Why a Rose Has Thorns

Thorns protect the rose
season after season from
intrusion from those who only
appreciate its outer beauty
and discard it when the
leaves begin to fall and the
inner beauty is exposed

The Heart and Soul of Africa

My heart belongs to Africa
Her essence brought my soul
back to the motherland
I walked on earth that already
recognized my footprints,
planted seeds in fertile soil and heard the music of
my ancestors in her voice

She wore the confidence of every
woman that raised me
I took her hand and carried her through fire
as repentance for all the sisters
and brothers that I couldn't
love while I was waiting for her

She spoke in tongues that made me feel invincible
Made me want to protect her and her entire village
Rule like the kings and queens
that were my ancestors
before colonialism tried to hunch their backs
and break their spirits

Africa reclaimed my heart
Beckoned me to return to my roots
Asked for my forgiveness
Forgave all my past transgressions
and gave me back my crown

The Caretaker

I stay ready just in
case she needs me
Ready to be a lover
or a fighter,
a fixer or a healer,
a listener or a problem-solver
If she is lonely,
I want to be there for her
Fill any void in her heart
Wipe out any darkness
with my light
Watch her smile as I work
Watch her exhale as each
burden is lifted
She may need me
and that is ok with me

Strong Sisters Unite

My sisters, we are standing in the quicksand of
political, racial, relationship and
other societal dysfunctions
Bravely declaring our strength and struggling to
hold it together but at what cost
We have nothing to prove; let us
protect our minds & bodies

Our strength is being used against us
Our ability to be the fixer in every situation masks
our humanity, our femininity, our vulnerability
Let's not wait until we can't
breathe to try to escape;
if we delay the healing, our
scars will be permanent

The world knows that we are strong because
our strength is legendary
We are Harriet Tubman, Michelle
Obama, and Rosa Parks
We are Oprah Winfrey, Nanny, and Mae Jameson
We are Shirley Chisholm, Portia
Simpson and Maya Angelou
We have birthed a nation, rescued
slaves, built empires,
traveled to space and written our place in history

Survival is not enough; we were built to rise
Let us take each other's hand in love and support
Embrace our vulnerabilities
Embrace our humanity
Heal our hearts and minds
Escape from negativity is not failure

Don't Try Me Today

Peace is a gift
but it is not free
Recognize its value
It was bought and sold
Packaged with pain and sacrifice
Honor the sacrifice
Don't lose your peace
today over what will be
a footnote in your life tomorrow
Save any disruption of the soul
for things of consequence
that will rock your world and
cause a shift in the universe

Therapy

Heart laid bare
Secrets no longer hidden
Opened to cleanse
Exposed to purify
Karma visited and
found no sins left to
be atoned.

Falling Leaves

Winter reluctantly surrenders to Spring
but the ground under her feet remains cold
her rosebuds sharpen their thorns and
are defiant in their refusal to bloom
choosing to hide until summer is done
scorching every life form in its path
but Autumn is her season
both the majestic oak and the timid flower
display their strength and beauty
shedding leaves with wild abandon
boldly laying themselves bare
changing colors to match their mood
it is the only change that gives her hope that
she too can survive another brutal Winter

We are Black Women: See Us

Take 2 steps closer
Extend your hand
Touch our hearts
Feel our spirits
We are fearful,
yet we are strong
We are vulnerable,
yet we are resilient
Our hearts break easily,
yet we love deeply
We are human
See our humanity
See us

Her King

She is not passive but she is peaceful
She is strong but she has vulnerabilities
She wants to be the boss at the office
but not the boss of you.

Bring her your strength
Empower her
She wants to feel your masculinity
Grow taller around her

Inhabit the earth, reach for the sky
Show her your power
Spread your feathers like the male bird
Make your inner beauty shine for her

Her shoulders are already heavy,
so just for tonight,
leave your insecurities at the door
Don't shed empty tears around her,
unless you plan to catch them
and use them to water her spirit,
her dreams, your love for her,
your passion for only her

Allow her to exhale in your presence

Pretty Words

He rides in, heart ablaze,
swinging the emotional rope,
pulling you in
with sweet words,
feeding your soul
with praise and adoration,
catapulting you high in the air
so that you are no longer grounded
in the reality
that words are enchanting
but love requires action;
it demands that you
descend from the clouds,
engage the hands and
work tirelessly & consistently
on the business of loving
Words & feelings blow in the wind,
loving takes a steady heart & hand

Accepting the Challenge
to Go High

Love and peace are needed in challenging times
Not just personal peace but taking concrete steps
to ensure the peace and safety of our community
We spring from one great tree of life so when our
actions are rooted in peace and love, we all thrive
The moment that we begin to
feel superior to another,
our roots weaken and we start
to lose our humanity
Let us not be afraid to face fear with love
Always remember that love
trumps every form of hate
One love. One heart. One blood. One human race
When they go low, we go so high
that we are unshakable

Lukewarm Life

Not rejecting
Not embracing
The water is still
Not freezing the soul
Not heating up the heart
Occasional ripples
to offer hope
that quickly fades
And still, a small voice
whispers — you deserve
more than a lukewarm life

Not Compatible

You are beautiful, kind, loving
and blessed with many gifts
but you are not the girl for him
Don't hang your self-esteem on
the temperamental sea of his desires;
you are not food for his insecurities
Move on to a love whose heart leaps
with joy when you enter the room
Don't look back
Don't wonder why

99 Hours of Therapy

99 hours of therapy
cracked open my pride
forced me to realize that
right becomes wrong when
a reckoning occurs
after midnight
with an angry heart
with alcohol in system
with scissors in hand

99 hours of self-flagellation
Therapist become pastor
Pastor become savior
Saved by finally believing that
mistakes were made
God understands
I can forgive myself
I am human

Come Home

I look at your photo often to see
the secrets behind your eyes
Your inner child calls out to me
Asks me to love and protect you
Tells me that you are silently fighting
demons that you don't
believe that I can understand
Nighttime soldier
Weekend warrior
Prayers are said for you
Tears are shed for you
My bones ache to love you
Go to battle for you
Protect the child
Love and respect the man
No judgment
Come home

The Abuser

You say that you want a strong woman
Strong enough to bear your burdens
Handle your drama
Fix your problems
but not strong enough to
Stand up for herself
Walk away

Yet, you don't respect her
because she
Handles your drama
Fixes your problems
Pretends to believe your lies
Love you in your weak places
Stay ride or die

The strong woman's only weakness is you

Follow the Love

Follow the love
It is a peaceful path
There is no climbing up dangerous terrain,
battling dragons and demons along the way,
carefully tiptoeing over hidden landmines

Follow the love
It doesn't hurt
You don't have to change yourself to receive it
It accepts that you are perfectly made
No permission is needed to travel
confidently in its world

Follow the love
You will recognize it by its non-resistance,
its warm embrace,
its offer for you to abide in its presence,
its sheer joy in being found

Love is No Longer Being Served

Remember when you were the world to her
When you felt her happiness level increase
when you walked into the room
When your words moved her soul
When your smile was everything to her
When you looked into her eyes and only
saw love and respect
She is gone now
but when you find that kind of
love again, treasure it
Treasure her

Riding and Dying

Return home
The door has been open
for far too long
It is getting hard to keep
the burglars out the house
and the trespassers off your lawn
You are fighting the world,
fighting your demons
while the place where your
love and acceptance reside
is crumbling without you
While you are out riding.
your home is dying
Return home to love

The Princess Takes the High Road

Believing all the fairytales,
she waited patiently for her prince to return.
She continued on the low road
for as long as she could
before realizing that the high road
was the only way to rise;
the only path to the castle.
She sharpened her weapons,
slayed through the self-doubt,
cut the fear from her heart, and
trimmed all the edges that were
blocking her vision.

With a clear vision, she wrote her own ending
"The princess bravely scaled
the walls of the castle.
As she rose to the top, she created
a path for the other
young ladies who would follow,
and placed a beacon
on the top of the castle to light their path
The End."

Women at Work

There are no idle hands in the pursuit
of Justice and Equality
We will finish the work of our elders and ancestors
who worked tirelessly to blaze a
trial with sweat and tears
We will care for our elders who fought for us,
write their stories, and share them
with each generation
so that we always remember on
whose shoulders we stand
We will not be passive in the face of injustice
and allow every generation to fight the same battles
We will drive our communities
to the polls and vote like
the lives of our children depend on it because it does

We will rewrite the history books so that our children
know that it didn't all begin with slavery
but with kings and queens
We will reject the derogative names that
broke the hearts of our ancestors
We will buy and build and own
and leave a financial legacy
We will raise our children to reject mediocrity
We will continue to speak for those who were silenced,
marginalized, and those whose
dreams remains deferred
There are no idle hands in the pursuit of Justice

Hu 'Man' Nature

Men have a reputation of being drama free
Selfishness isn't considered drama
It doesn't scream or throw a punch
but it is the quiet killer of the soul
It takes without gratitude
It loves only when it is convenient
and scolds her for expecting more
The resulting heartbreak feels self-inflicted
as he moves on effortlessly
leaving her to untangle all the invisible
emotional strings that were attached to his love

The Secret

whispers
from my mouth
to God's ear
to your heart
a promise of
agape love where
old wounds heal
cracks in the foundation
of your soul are filled
in all the barren places
where hope was lost
before the secret was
revealed and fear died
leaving us to finally
smell the roses that the
lucky ones have been
playing with so recklessly

A Prayer and a Plan

God realized that I was on the verge
of drowning and threw me a lifeline
I kept reaching for it but over and over,
again, it slipped through my fingers
But he has never given up on me
so I never give up on me
My sisters, keep praying, keep trusting
keep reaching
You are not alone

Courage is Our Legacy

Sometimes, we step out on a limb and fall
Discouraged, we contemplate how
bravery was so harshly rewarded,
wonder which step sealed our fate
Bravery is a single act of courage
and it doesn't tell the full story
Courage powers us from deep inside
It wills us to shake off the disappointment,
push on through, blaze a new trail
Remember the path that our ancestors paved
Bravery isn't always rewarded but we
have a history of courage and our courage
will be the final chapter in our story

The Strength of a Single Mother

Your shoulders are heavy,
but you stand tall and raise your head high,
knowing that you are raising kings and queens,
future leaders of the world

You are pounding the pavement,
kicking butt, making it look easy
but we know better;
we know the struggle,
we understand the pain

You are sometimes joyful
sometimes fearful,
saying quiet prayers,
crying silent tears,
working miracles with limited resources

We see you,
We respect you
We are proud of you,
We have your back
The road feels lonely
but you are not alone

To My Mother

You are the wind at my back
Footprints in the sand when I am lost
Carefully holding the ladder as I climb
Gathering the cheering section
Arms open to meet me at the end of every race
First to throw the confetti when I win
Hugs, tears, ready to fight, if needed when I lose
You are my mother - showing
stedfast love and support
Quietly doing God's work without complaint
I am overcome with gratitude

Strong. Black. Woman

Hold on to a shred of dignity
Scream inside
Let the tears fall behind closed doors
You are your mama's child
and she is a proud black woman

She would be disappointed
if she knew that your heart breaks so easily
That you blow in the wind
when she raised you to be strong

Strong. Black. Woman
Each word is non-negotiable,
so swallow hard,
steady yourself,
and carry on

Black Girls Don't Cry is a Lie

Vulnerability inspires fear
so they tell you that the world
doesn't want to see a bleeding heart
There is no empathy for black damsels
in distress so hold it all in, tears cause a mess
to the narrative of the strong black woman
Sisters, your emotions is your currency
Never fear the ugly cry
Are you needy? Hell, yes!
Wear your heart in your hands and
your emotions on your sleeves
Black girls don't cry has been the biggest lie

Vulnerable Souls

There are vulnerable souls
hiding under decaying skin,
pain eating away at the flesh,
fighting its way through the pores
desperate to escape the
confines of a society
that rewards strength
when we all start vulnerable
on the inside

Life with a Narcissist

To love without fear is
tomorrow's prayer
but tonight brings
emotional eggshells, and
machiavellian use of power
Existing under a microscope with
each move measured
One delicate step forward is the crown
Two bold steps is the dungeon
Those are tonight's rules
Tomorrow the rules change
and the game with my heart begins again

I See a King

I am in love with God's original plan
He intended for you to be a better man
Innocence stolen in a distant land
But your blueprint wasn't written in the sand
The universe held it tightly in its hands

The world says not to fall in love
with a shadow of a man
Living life selfishly with no vision or destination
I only see greatness in your eyes
I see your truth in the midst of all your lies
Look at your reflection through
my eyes and you will see
The king that the universe designed you to be

Dalvey Girl

Take me back to the innocence of primary school
where joy was sitting under a mango tree
playing ring around the rosie with the girls
rolling marbles with the boys
playing hopscotch, spinning gig
always the brown girl in the ring
reliving the good times
before any innocence was lost
when the slate was clean every day
and joy was in learning, playing, living
in the sweet land of my birth

No Place to Hide

At birth,
we open our eyes,
anxiously
looking to be held,
hoping to be loved
Vulnerability
starts at birth
Often the outstretched
arms never appear
and the anxiety
never disappears
We wrap our arms
around ourselves
hoping and praying
that it is enough

Reclaim Your Heart

I was in the valley of despair,
waiting,
hoping,
praying
that you would see my worth,
that this would be the day
that you would acknowledge that I am your light

I was not alone in the valley
I found sisters with
dashed hopes,
deferred dreams,
fallen crowns,
self-inflicted wounds
existing in a broken place—
alive but not living

Sisters,
look up, reach up!
Your crowns are damaged but not broken
Shake off the self-hate
Grab hold of self-worth
and walk out of the valley of despair

Your walk may be unsteady but you won't fall
Robe your self-esteem in royal garments
Fiercely guard it from the enemy
of loneliness, self-doubt
Don't look for permission or validation to shine
Bow to the reflection in your own mirror
Reclaim your heart

Other People's Business

Sometimes, we accidentally stumble into
drama and refuse to look away
Refuse to be pulled aways to safety
We dive in to save those who did not ask to be
saved and do not appreciate our intervention
Self-sacrificing moths to the flame of fire that
was not intended to consume us
Sister-friend, walk away

Naked

They don't understand why I stay with you
because they don't see my soul when it is not
buried under jewelry and weaves
and designer clothes
With you, I am perfectly imperfect;
you see all of me,
you know my secrets, you love my nakedness
We are both broken in ways that
make us a perfect fit
We are safe with each other;
on the outside there is dysfunction
but within these walls, we have found home

The Limit

It is the tiny
slights
that hurt
the most
Sometimes
one extra
drop of
water can
cause the
dam to
overflow
You don't
know what
your limit is
until you
reach it

Protection

She is an empath
all heartbreakers
swipe left
Can't trust you
not to break
all the beauty that
is inside of her

Girls Trip

Soulmates are friends
whose spirits travel together,
hearts break and mend together,
and souls rise together in love
acceptance and harmony

Girl, Create Your Own Magic

The magician hypnotized her
and then walked away
Off to live his best life
while she spends her days staring
into the face of the sun
She didn't blame him for the burn
She learned not to trust a street performer
She learned that she had the power to
create her own magic

Sister. Friend. Angel

God sent me an angel
beautiful
vibrant
badass
ride or die friend
soul sister
party starter
loyal to her core
slaying life and motivating
me to do the same

Innocence Lost #BlackGirlsMatter

Eyes squeezed tightly
to avoid the face of evil
Bruises from her fingernails
penetrating her skin
Weight that she is too young to carry
Mind drifting to escape her
present circumstances
Waiting for her savior
Abandoning all hopes of a savior
Willing courage from her chest to
her throat and out her mouth
to speak her truth

Words sending shockwaves that
reverberates resulting in
exploding anger and fear
that hits her in the heart
No empathy or understanding, just
doubting
shaming
silencing
Alone, she falls to her knees and
prays for no more pain
Prayers granted but
innocence already stolen
Faith in humanity lost

The Blueprint for your Life

If you have lost your way
Return home
Study the blueprint for your life
Remember your hopes and dreams
Rewrite the narrative that binds you
Add cherished child, abundantly blessed adult
Erase the spirit of rejection and abandonment
Set aside broken hearts and dashed hopes
Close the door on professional failures and
everything else that is weighing your soul down
Clear the self-defeating clutter from
your mind and return to love; it is the only word
that the universe wrote next to your name.

Our Genesis

Searching for a feeling
the one that makes me
feel invincible
dancing
chanting
glory hallelujah
thanking God for what is now
and what is to come
stepping with purpose
walking with the angels
through fear and hate and fury
and storms and tsunami and
volcanic eruptions
that were intended to kill the seeds
that were planted in our being
the ones that gave us dominion
over all living things.

Embrace the Sun

To the sun, you are everything
To the clouds, you will never be enough
Stop chasing the clouds in your life
You don't have to chase the sun, it will find you
Just have faith and walk towards the light

Free the Mind

Be mindful of negativity
Negative thoughts become obsessions
Obsessions become deep emotions
Emotions become painful
Pain becomes cancerous to the body
Free the mind from poison

Hurricane Season of Love

The day the hurricane came I was alone
It brought a powerful lesson about love
Infatuation goes dormant in times of a storm
Lust withers
They both send thoughts and prayers from afar

Love stands by your side
Hands ready to do the heavy lifting
Ready to
Share the fear
Be your anchor as the wind blows
Curl up under the blanket with you
Pick up the pieces after the storm
Joyful that together you made it through

Sis, Finally!

Just like that, everything that I thought
was wrong with me become an asset
I looked in the mirror and realized that I
am perfect just the way that God made me
I struggled because I have been standing
in the wrong room with the wrong people
Trying to fit in, looking for approval, asking
for permission to be authentically me

My sisters, if you are still struggling, wipe your
tears so that you can see the beauty that is inside
Find your tribe, your sister circle,
your prayer warriors

Clothe yourself in self-love and
self-acceptance, believe
that you are enough; watch the
pieces of your mirror come
together to finally reflect all the
beauty that is in your heart

Down But Never Out

Every, single day
there are people
coming back from
the depths of addiction
and abuse and
unimaginable suffering
and rising higher
than the world expects
breaking chains
fighting for others
pulling their friends up
sometimes fearless
often being courageous
in the midst of fear
don't give up on anyone
don't give up on you

Self-Medicating

There is nothing
behind her eyes
No happiness
No sadness
No joy
No pain
No anxiety
No peace
She drinks all the
pain away
But it also leaves
her soul empty and
longing to be refilled
with more poison.

Drowning in Feelings

I know that it is a painful time for you
but the world needs your heart to begin healing
Outside of your feelings await
a world that needs you
You have a beautiful heart and so much love to give
There are talents that the universe
has bestowed on only you
You may not die from a broken
heart but it robs you of
your ability to be a blessing to
others and to enjoy all
the blessings that the universe has in store for you
You are more powerful than the pain
running through your veins
You are more powerful than the
thoughts consuming your mind
Step out of the shadows and create
your footprints in the sand

Her Undoing

As she took his hand
the rain started falling but
the sun was still shining
So she let her guards down
from her leaves to her root
That was her undoing
Strong trees fall hard
Shocked to hit the ground
She had weathered so many
powerful storms, only to be toppled
by the trickery of a summer shower

Church

Walls crumbling
Heart failing
Strength waning
Knees caving
Dreams ending

After the Choir Sings

Chains breaking
Anchor holding
Lessons learning
Hope rising
Rebirth happening

How I Met Your Father

She saw him walk in alone
anxiously looking around the room
for a familiar face, looking out the window
like a child hoping for a surprise

He lowered his head when the nurse asked
Who is your emergency contact?
Is there anyone that you can call?
You can't go into surgery alone

I am a strong black man, I don't need anyone
I walked over, touched his shoulder
and said, "I am here for him."
Sometimes, for better or worse has
to start with being there for the worse

Shades of Pink

It never dawned on her
that she could love a woman
more than she loved herself;
she thought that that kind of
insane love was reserved for men

Church Girl

She was perched on a high horse
Trying to live the life of a Proverbs 31 girl
willingly walking with the chains
that started in Sunday school
each link a measure of her worth
more links, more worth
more links, more heaviness
collapsing under the pressure
of expectations and judgment

Years on the ground, freeing herself
link by link, deprograming, learning
to breathe again, to speak from her heart,
to act without asking for approval
Forgetting everything they ever told her
to do, to say, to be. Empowered to
write her own story in the good book

Stop in the Name of Love

Don't come back
Just because you can
Let me love again
I need to love again
That is how you show love
Understand
I need you to understand
That I need to be healthy again
To practice self-love again
That is love
Sometimes the love is in the leaving
Understand
Don't come back
Just because you can

Addiction

I look into your eyes and
no longer see my reflection
Every inch of your body is the same
but your mind is in your heaven
You smile and agree to everything because
you know that none of it matters
You are still my greatest high
but you are traveling higher
The love that I knew is lost
But you have found another love
Discovered new avenues in your brain
Living in a euphoria that I dare not imagine
I won't travel with you because life on earth
is too precious to me to risk it all
You no longer value your treasures here on earth
Earth has lost its power over you

Scars

Her heart is wild, her soul is peaceful
yet she writes about pain and anxiety
and vulnerability because she has been
in the battlefield, seen the carnage
Her scars are right below the surface
She writes to keep them there

Fear Surrenders

Walk courageously
No doubt
No fear
No self-sabotage
Allow yourself to
give love, feel love
BE love
until
fear surrenders

I am Who I Am

Self-acceptance
is a journey from
will they like me to
will I like them to
I am who I am
No judgment
No affirmation needed
I am enough

From One Sister to Another

There will be days when you wake up
and feel like you have nothing left to give
Listen to your body - rest, pray, exercise,
meditate, detox from anything unhealthy,
speak to a counselor, call a friend, write,
write, write your truth. Just know that you
are not as alone as you feel and more loved
than you know

Humanity Not For Sale

You are worthy
always have been
I see you
giving, serving, loving
until your cup is empty
Fueled by the need to please
Letting the takers of the world take
until you are hallow on the inside
It is time to reclaim your humanity
Chant, I am worthy, always have been
There is nothing else for me to prove
I am more than enough
It is time for me to exhale and just BE.

Love, Struggle and Resilience

Lest you get weary
Lest you lose faith and forget your magnificence
when faced with that other ism that resides
at the intersection of race and gender
Rest your soul on the shoulders
of your band of sisters
Black woman - feminist - womanist - fighter
Holding up two heavy banners for freedom and
passing them from generation to generation
because there is no cure for racism and sexism
Write the name of each soldier in the journal
of every black girl who needs to go into the world
armed with the fighting spirit of our heroes

Shirley Chisholm
Dorothy Height
Frances Ellen Watkins Harper
Ida B. Wells
Angela Davis

Audre Lorde
Pauli Murray
Mary Church Terrell
Sojourner Truth

...and the many other brave women who
gave meaning to the words — PROUD and BLACK
and WOMAN

Roar to Your Own Beat
Janet Autherine

About the Author

Janet has a heart for storytelling and for empowering women. She is the mother of three sons. She uses her journey from humble beginnings in Jamaica to an attorney and respected writer to inspire women to embrace their unique journey and boldly speak their truth.

She is the author of Growing into Greatness with God: 7 Paths to Greatness for our Sons & Daughters (youth), Wild Heart, Peaceful Soul (poetry) and Island Mindfulness: How to Use the Transformational Power of Mindfulness to Create an Abundant Life. Her books are available on Amazon. Follow her journey at www. janetautherine.com and IG: @JanetAutherine

Index

Mothers of Black Boys Don't Exhale 2

A Vulnerable Start to Life 4

The Soul of a Black Woman 5

Brown Girl Joy 6

Black Love 7

Hell No 8

You are Worthy 9

The Black Woman's Burden 10

Raise Hell 13

Girls Learn Early to Be Resilient 14

Clothed in Love 15

Breaking News! I am Above it All 17

Pour Love into the Offering Plate 19

A Mother's Prayer for her Gifted Sons 20

Selling Love in the Craft Market 22

Why a Rose Has Thorns 24

The Heart and Soul of Africa 25

The Caretaker 27

Strong Sisters Unite 28

Don't Try Me Today 30

Therapy 31

Falling Leaves 32

We are Black Women: See Us 33

Her King 34

Pretty Words 36

Accepting the Challenge to Go High 37

Lukewarm Life 38

Not Compatible 39
99 Hours of Therapy 40
Come Home 41
The Abuser.. 42
Follow the Love... 43
Love is No Longer Being Served 44
Riding and Dying... 45
The Princess Takes the High Road 46
Women at Work... 47
Hu 'Man' Nature.. 48
The Secret 49
A Prayer and a Plan 50
Courage is Our Legacy 51
The Strength of a Single Mother 52
To My Mother 54
Strong. Black. Woman.. 55
Black Girls Don't Cry is a Lie................................... 56
Vulnerable Souls 57
Life with a Narcissist... 58
I See a King.. 59
Dalvey Girl 60
No Place to Hide 61
Reclaim Your Heart 62
Other People's Business... 64
Naked 65
The Limit 66
Protection... 67
Girls Trip 68
Girl, Create Your Own Magic 69

Sister. Friend. Angel 70
Innocence Lost #BlackGirlsMatter 71
The Blueprint for your Life 73
Our Genesis 74
Embrace the Sun 75
Free the Mind 76
Hurricane Season of Love... 77
Sis, Finally! 78
Down But Never Out... 79
Self-Medicating 80
Drowning in Feelings.. 81
Her Undoing 82
Church... 83
How I Met Your Father.. 84
Shades of Pink 85
Church Girl.. 86
Stop in the Name of Love 87
Addiction 88
Scars 89
Fear Surrenders... 90
I am Who I Am 91
From One Sister to Another 92
Humanity Not For Sale 93
Love, Struggle and Resilience.. 94

Made in the USA
Middletown, DE
27 June 2022

67864839R00064